# IBIZA

*Love in words*

## Geetika Kaura

QUICK READS

*by Writersgram Publications*

IBIZA – Love In Words

*Poetry by* Geetika Kaura

First Impression: February 2020

© Geetika Kaura

**ISBN:** 978-9389244472

**Published by:** Writersgram Publications, New Delhi
www.writersgram.com
publications@writersgram.com

**Maximum Retail Price:** ₹ 180/-

Geetika Kaura asserts the moral right to be identified as the author of this book.

# A WORD FROM THE AUTHOR

I am like any dreamy girl in this world who purely believes magic dipped in hard work. Words are life to me. The way a person is mad for coffee, they cannot resist a day without coffee these words brew inside me every time. I took breathe I release an idea which vanishes after a while. Jokes apart!!

I write poetry to say what I can't talk. Instead of keeping it inside I spill it on paper and have believed, that day will come I will  spread my words in this world. Some words are harsh, some are tender, some came out of love, some out of hate. At times some out of pride, lust and other detachable emotions of life.

Initially I thought penning down my thoughts will take me to the world I want to live in as I came closer and closer to myself I became more awaken. I loved as an insane. Being loved and appreciated by people. I somehow managed to earn relationships which is indeed a jewel for my life. Like any girl I even got dumped for a reason, I got loved for a season, I understood what my mom means to me not just to write poetry but poetry allowed me to think about the things I never tried to imagine.

What a wonderful creation are these words sometimes said and rarely kept, sometimes kept without even said. Sometimes neither said nor kept just felt in the form of unrequited love, even this is not bad it has it's own pleasure.

Keeping in mind the beauteous things about life I am introducing my collection of feelings, a plethora a writings with you with a positive aspect that this may please you in the same it pleases me.

Here comes my "Ibiza"…

*Ibiza is a beautiful island in the Mediterranean sea off the east coast of Spain The same way this collection of my work is beautiful collection of pain and gain. Whenever my heart is heavy or it is so happy that it wants cuddle with a teddy, every emotion is here. Hope you enjoy it…*

# CONTENTS

# LET GO PINNACLE

Life gives reminders of losing time in many ways but we always ignore them as we all always pour a little to the things which are satanic for us.

Arrogance
Ego
Selfishness
Laziness
Gluttony
Jealousy
Impatience

We often forget that we are blessed in one way or another. And we can take advantage of the place we are in and take a deep breathe before we utter any word or start cursing are current situation because that is a fact. Our current situation is our journey not the destination. When I do so I feel a little more rejuvenated then give a slight positive start to upcoming time. That's how it works. Cursing is easy, austerity is rare.

# THE MIRROR

You can't take it, if I talk the way you do,
Moreover it is out of my league too,
I decided to carry a mirror whenever we meet,
See how treacherous the image is…

# ME AND MY DREAM

One silence is deliberately
Another is chosen
Both cries in parallel paths,
One seemed laughter but was not,
Another like slaughter and it was indeed…

# HICCUPS…

I'm leaving
this place
Still I have a lot to say,
to ask,
to rely,
There are possibilities,
There are questions,
before,
Moving on I think it's time to ask,
Anyway,
Some other time,
Some other day,
When you have heart to listen,
and time to stay,
If not now then
may be in another ours gloomy
grey day!

# RESTORING LOVE

Yesterday was a different starry night so shine;
Where little was delight and little was whine;
I'm just a corp living a life to redefine in every possible style;
Here 'to live' actually means to revive
every single moment of time,
Some of me, some for the people I love,
Also opening my arms wide open,
To the modern relations that too are divine,
I'll  too keep the older ones stable and make my love outshine even
it will take all of trying,
All this might take every bit of me to love to be determined
I this understood now not as a child but like a strong spine,
In this life we can't leave everything to live life in our own
conformity
Some things are to be done for the honey without any burden,
On the tiny wings of this bee,
Give and take is not always a barter,
It's also a glee,
Which makes the love stays…

# RARE LOVE

He was giving his dying wife little jokes and hiccups
Leaning at the bay of terrace
Thinking life is beautiful as a rose flower,
Just like carrying thorns at the bottom,
Every passing hour isn't autumn,
The essence of grey is also part of life
It just matter to a slight
Then why keep on whining,
Try to choose to be little more shining,
Roses have thorns for a reason,
Life too has pain for a reason,
Else how'll you see colours of changing seasons.
We have lessons from past which is indeed not to broadcast,
Keeping the experience in mind let the life move on coz it is meant
to go on.
Be your own Cupid even if it asks you dance in middle of the night
in absence of light,
Think at that moment how to be fastidious enough,
Not letting that juvenile die,
Even if there is grey sky as the day will soon come when the grey
sky will gleam.
So be mad, be carefree, make the beautiful more beautified.
Let the stones in your way turn into bed of roses,
Till then keep walking with heads up…
Raise the toast and drink your cup…
Rest whatever is happening around is God's setup…

# OLD BRIDGE WHERE LOVERS MEET

It is 2 am,
No sign of sleep goddamn,
The night for her is never over,
As black clouds are just forever,
Never mind to smile quintessentially?
It is what ?
Nothing more!
Walking across the shore.
Crossing the small ancient bridge.
where many lovers meet!
Strange is that there only
On the point solely,
Evidence of reunite,
Now there the most essential relation of her life
Just died !
How will she decide?
Who will her guide?
Mom or dad…

As they took their final decision.
And kept just one condition,
Some days it's her others it's him,
Thought made her lips little prim…
The first time ever
She thought the human relations are too perplex.

# THE WARMTH OF YOU...

In a temporarily artificial world,
Beneath the tree,
Far away from the army,
Of fast pacing faces,
with permanent smiling jaws,
You give me the real lifted crescent under my nose,
As you lift me and wrap me around,
The warmth is worthy,
And it's a charismatic journey…

# SETBACKS OR CATAPULTS...

The way you talk, the way you look,

The way you walk is indeed act as a magnet to many but what makes that person to be in your life for long or for forever is the way you think !!

We often talk about love and happiness as synonyms to each other and yes that's true they are well in relationship yet that relationship isn't something you find in outer world. It is inside you smiling like a child when you see yourself in the mirror in someone's eyes.

Temporary setbacks are inevitable yet they aren't a permanent way of life. What we need is optimistic way of thinking and reflection of the same.

I'm done with complaining about the missing things and a sudden realisation that what was not complete was me nothing else. Smiling in pictures and crying when alone gathered emotions to that extent that when in public I enjoy my own company that indeed made me brave but for a time being I realised that it is nothing but a temporary bad phase which will pass but definitely it will change me and I'll make sure for a better one.

# LOVE TONIGHT

Tonight,
My knight,
Let's not stay out of sight,
Despite,
All the miles we are apart,
I'm sure that's not only my plight,
We are the same,
Let's make schemes,
Instead of cries and also the screams,
Let's make them happen,
Our dreams,
We are apart,
Not us,
That's what make us beloved,
There is a cord,
Which ties our heart,
Not everyone can afford
This love  need not to be shoved…

# NEVER PLANNED THAT POISONED DREAM

Since when these were fatal breasts,
It's really hard to digest,
Since when that parasite infest,
Now I'm thinking,
Before,
I least concern,
We made love,
Little kinky also,
Yet pure as a holy water,
Now that each dream has been shattered,
Realizing I have spent my life not more than in earning,
Me bread,
Or not just bread ,
Actually busy in making life more beautiful,
Each time thinking of little more pennies,
Now when we think to give birth to a newborn,
The time came now is just to mourn,
These breasts would never feed,
Would never feel a tender touch,
As the pain so much,
Since when these breasts were fatal breasts,
That I'm counting my days,
In the age of counting hours spent in craze,
Alas ! these breasts were fatal,
I wish I could have got the chance of fighting the battle,
I wish I could have got the chance of fighting the battle…
I wish my last days I can devote to charity,
Rather than just dealing with this chemotherapy…

# DIMENSIONS

Be the girl as delicate as petals of rose,
Be the girl as harsh as grating coos of crows,
Be the love spiller to the rough universe,
Be the hate reflector too in the scenario worse,
Essential it is for the self esteem,
Specifically when love is turning way too mainstream,
Be the bitch who wears black as it gives current to some,
Carry the heart filled with peace of white where all hate could
succumb.

Wherever you go be the life of that place,
No matter what is the phase…

Take care of yourself no one else will do,
Shine and rise each day with the gait of pride,
Make sure that pride is not that one which some lied
On the name of honor
You are the bold innocence
Who can be defiance to the enemies.

# GREY...

Doomed in grey, hate grey because it brings or symbolises sadness. Dude it's not the colour it's the cover which is there on your way of living life. Just crossing paths walking on grass I was pondering why we link colours with our emotions, red anger or danger, green harmony, grey gloomy, am I mad ??

I love grey and black than any other colours. As I think it's all about perception. Grey is even the colour of love making, it's even the colour of subtle abstract art.

I don't know how many people will read this just want to pour my heart out feeling that one should not disseminate just their perspective or ideas. Doing that is cool just be open to accept others perspective too. Can you be happy in greys too ?

Close your eyes to find the answer...

# PROFOUND THINKING

Stand there
Quite in a ponder
Stand there a bit longer
Enough of criticism
For a moment it's good to follow chauvinism,
This time the boundary in which your soul lies
If bad then good also resides,

Stand there a little longer
To appreciate
Else the outer criticism is enough to hinder your confidence and
your value to depreciate

Make a list of things you love about yourself as I made it today,
Things are ample,
I ain't ashamed of it to ramble.

More importantly I always love everything a little more,
Without measurements or guidelines,
It's ok if I get hit by porcupines
That's my way
And I'm proud of it that I'm not leaning on an ashtray…

# I ASKED MYSELF WHY I LOVE YOU SO MUCH ?

I close my eyes and let them rest for a while
You are entering my life with rainbow colours,
Doing things I never expect because they always left me in wonder
that I love you so much
First answer came that's it's you who love me too much
Then the most beauteous thing about you that your love never woes
In fact it let me love me a little more
Accept me the way I'm
Bit of socially wanderer
The other part is complete home maker
You let me open my heart out every now and then,
And when drama reaches its pinnacle
You still make room for it to let it settle.
In the world full of fake promises, strange lies and broken ties, you
are the one who gives me butterflies
In the room full with people
You catch my attention
And I feel sensation
Just when you are around
This is not it, I have many more appreciation but you need no
apprehension
Just be with me as this
I can walk on thorns as I know you'll make them roses for me
Even if sometimes it won't be possible then I'll walk on it even if it
will pain
Life being alone never was a plane for me

So walking alone anymore will not be a glee and it won't set me
free
Let's be together
In chatter and also in worst of mood swings
Let's hold each other's hands and also our hearts with invisible
strings
You are for me what I deserve
I'll for you what you'll preserve
I'll sing the love hymn for you now and till eternity.

# IMAGES IN MOTIONS

People click pictures
when they meet,
I personally adore the idea as it's
important for memory
When present fades,
And you'll be at some other street
Yet some moments don't need to be seized
with the camera
As these eyes are an almirah,
Of many moments,
That don't have negatives,
To develop
still they are inscribed till eternal gallop…

# TRAVELLING

I turned twenty-five
I decided to make decisions less indecisive,
with all cautious thoughts and attention
And I started seeing my life enliven,
Since then 3 years have passed and every morning I wake up in
order to take new lessons and the older ones just to recall,
I took a yellow and black taxi,
which drove me to that jamun tree
Where I left my initial 5 years of childhood,
Turning the pages of my recent novel I refreshed me playing with
my grandpa's beard,
All the good teaching of his now make sense to me and make my
more cleared,
Thinking this I parked my I20,
where my family now preparing to make me bride,
I then took the ascenseur,
the moment it shuts it doors I recalled my cathartic pride
of struggles and pain showed like a see-saw
And then I opened the door with my hands and it seemed a little
more struggle
I belonged to that future where everything is mechanized
Amidst of hand opening lifts and automatic things to real time
lovers to passionate one night stands,
I left my home to see the unseen places as a friendless wanderer
where I learnt most of the lessons without any chalk talk
To make all adjustments and not just to crib that my milk ain't have
bournvita

which no book can tell
keen observation and becoming a sapien who only craves for life,
love and laughter.
And also keeping the kid inside alive,
from now, mostly I should behave like senorita.
In my timeline before I touch thirty.
While opening the door of my time machine I find a way to bejewel
my pride, courage, hard work to the next shore where my future
will shine bright.

# AKS...

अभी तक कहते है मुझे अक्स तेरा

पर माँ कोई ख़ास शक्स तो नही हूँ बस यही कि

जब आज अपने कोमल हाथों में जवाब ढूँढता है कि तेरे हाथ खुरदरे क्यू है ?

जो आज आवाज़ ऊँची हो तो जानता है कि कोई नही है सहनेवाला और तब

भी इतना प्यार करनेवाला

शकल का मिलना जन्म से आम बात है

पर सीरत का मिलना जीवन का धीरज तेय करता हैं

और यही एक नायाब चीज़ ही तो मैंने तुमसे है पायी


सब कहते है सूरत ही भी हमारी हर चीज़ मिलती है

हँसी, तेवर, गुस्सा यहाँ तक माथे की सिलवट

पर एक दूसरे के लिए जो प्यार और विश्वास है वो कुछ ख़ास है

कभी कभी भगवान से कितना लड़ती हो फिर छिपकर थोड़ा सा रो लेती हो

खाना खाने के लिए बचपन में मैंने जितना सताया है अब सारे बदले गिनगिन

कर लेती हो

बचपन में कदम उठाना सिखाया

अब पूरी ज़िद करके मोबाइल पे उँगलिया चलाकर दिखाया

फिर जब मैं खुद से पूछती हूँ कि माँ तुम ऐसी क्यू हो

माँ तुम माँ हो ना। इसीलिए शायद ऐसी हो


बचपन से हर डुप्पट्टे से साड़ी बनाकर खेली

तुम्हारा मुझे ज़ोर से डाँटना फिर एकदम गले से लगालेना

माँ तुम हो ना ख़ास और मेरे लिए सबर का बांध

बिना वपिसी में कुछ चाहे तुम्हें देखा है हमेशा सिर्फ़ प्यार करते हुए

तभी ना ये सारी दुनिया की निगाहे एक तरफ़ तुम्हारे हाथों की ठंडी छाँहें

एक तरफ़...

# AISLE BEFORE WAKE UP AS BRIDE

A thin hair strand on my neck
The ticklish feeling at midnight
Some more lonesome sleepless nights,
Beautiful days are not much far from our sights
These days will soon pass borrowing wings of some flight
And bring us together like a titanic pose on the deck
Drowning in each other's eyes,
Where we both seize the time
And discuss these moments we spent in planning
then make love without any prior warning…

# IS IT TOO LATE ?

To decide not to take part in the parade ?
Where liars are participating in disguise.
Bearing wounds given by then ain't a surprise.
Be me is my mantra to be precise.
Restricting and retreating is needed I realise
 Is it too late ?
To decide not to take part in the parade ?
Spending hours making memories with the ones I love
They thinkin this is what I deserve!
Walking-in and leaving when they want
Giving my shoulder them to cry
Who is there when it's the thing need I ?
Recipient of the compliment you are a strong woman without a
lie…
But that doesn't make you any high
Even in single sight of my eye…
Is it too late ?
To decide not to take part in the parade ?
The ones are gone may they stay bless
The ones will come will have an access
To the new me without a mess…

# NUMB AND PAUSE

Numb is present, yet the pause I applause.
Pause is when we saw each other, filled the life with vibrant colour,
Numb I am, realising it's hard to recover.

Pause is when you kissed my forehead,
and we took those vows for the life ahead,
Numb I am, realising it's hard to recover.

Pause is when we had our first fight,
and the first apology you write,
In this moment, while reading it,
Numb I am realising it's hard to recover.

Pause I am in the moment we had spent as lovers,
Numb I am to find there is nothing left to discover.

# LOG KYA KAHENGE

He belongs to the minority where people think he can't do charity,
In reality, that teenager knows only love to entail with,
But their group forbids him to prevail it,
By the fear throughout life that "log kya kahenge"
She turned 25, and the search begin,
Before that she whole solely loved her from out and within,
But now she has to lose weight to fittin,
Before that numerous rejections should ramble the phrase followed
by your aren't bride for him,
And with her the fear stays throughout that "log kya kahenge"
Men shouldn't express, as it will definitely a pity
"Aisa to log kahenge" to the groom who is getting married soon.
But he and she know it's the most romantic thing when you aren't
with a troupe and with 'the one' and bedded
Phir kya parwah "Kya log kahenge"
Many dreams were killed till date
Success are those who changed their fate
By letting go this silly phrase
And end up going behind what they want to chase
"Log kya kahenge" when you leave your studies and start following
your passion
Could be writing day and night be happy or in plight
Initially they were these log who said no one will give sight
As the trend these days is of tok-tik and musically
Who else is finicky, to read, read and read
Knowing only I that this gives me strength of living and myself to
breed in all possible way.

"Log to bas kahenge" par ab hum ye "aur na sochenge"
Also I found myself becoming these log once for a while but capable was I to take me out of it.
As I knew I was not the one to judge sinner sinning a bit differently, constantly and hauntingly.

# REVIVE

It stuck in my mind suddenly what transformed me. The girl who loves to be surrounded by many suddenly my own company is a blessing for me. That doesn't mean that I don't like to meet people and my friends it's just that due to some jiff with like I spent some good quality time in my own company. Having sips of my bitter coffee makes me realise that life isn't equally bitter there are umpteenth things to adore, colour to fill your life with just we need to remove those old glasses because they are full of mist which doesn't allow to see any farther. People will come and go, moments will happen some we capture, some we delete. Some deleted yet imprinted as an everlasting memory but does it mean we should cut ourselves from the world because things aren't going well nowadays. No matter what the situation is it's you standing for you if you have someone as a backbone like father mother or husband that's pretty cool but remember one time will come they also want their personal time. Maybe they don't say directly but you will feel it. I don't know why I'm writing this just pondering in my thoughts scribble some thoughts on paper.

*Cheers to thing called life!*

# THAT LOVE IS NOT LOVE !

And that was the love which couldn't love her with screams!
And that was the love she saw in dreams…
And that was the love she touched with fingertips,
And that was the love happened with the collision of gypsies and hippies,
And that was the love that helped her regain,
There her miseries did abstain,
She felt the same lame game left with…
Once again…

# THE SOUVENIR

I dropped a glass souvenir,
It was gifted,
My feelings drifted,
To and fro
Towards a deep path,
With narrow and dark ending,
And I laughed so hard,
That I dated a sociopath,
The pieces were so tiny,
For a moment I felt whiny,
Remembering the words "I'm yours forever"
And I trusted it blindly,
It pierced the tip of my thumb,
Blood overflowed and I was numb,
Probably not to stop loving,
But to continue showering,
More on myself than on you…

# GAY IN A METRO…

Red was the colour on his lips, cheeks and fingertips,
Was adequate to make men stand with hand on their hips,
Both of them laughing at each other,
And the laugh was becoming loud one after another,
They were laughing at the epicene,
Unknowingly that he can be the lethal gene,
He has the guts to stand on what he is,
Not like them happy in the world imitative,
Mocking at the indestructible spirit,
Transforming it into a spear hit…

# THE REQUITED MOTHER…

Love is a mere feeling,
it is a process of two hearts sealing,
People think those two hearts are always a girl and a guy,
not all of them are as pretty as a pearl.
This time it was different,
It came into existence out of perseverance,
She is the mother
nothing but his smile can bother,
No accusations, no blames, is her preference,
She has learnt the life of endurance,
Every morning is more beautiful,
When he kisses on her forehead,
No more worries can spoil,
her peace she said…

# THE BREAKTHROUGH

The love is precious
When the feelings are audacious,
Yet the conspiracies of heart and soul,
Won on a day she reverted in the same way,
Indeed she was being broken,
in tiny pieces from inside,
Perhaps he'll take this step of hers offensive,
for her own confidence it was apprehensive,
Ample succumbed thus she chide,
Yet a part of hers left behind,
Since his action neither unkind nor defined…

# LIVE IT BEFORE IT SHALL PASS…

Nothing is there beyond this,
Happiness,
Love,
Life,
Pain,
Lies,
Trust,
All is true, yet concealed,
She knows nothing resilient
It is that one moment,
Let it be permanent in this jiff,
Think later, and let it happen,
This beat shall pass,
Live it, like thunder of one hand clappin…

# THE CHOSEN BOUNDARY...

It revolves around my heart,
yet the feel is missing,
I can see it, but can't catch it,
that is numb me,
for me love is always that way,
all the times it comes but never stay,
though it is a beautiful array...
standing on my doorway,
Encore holding a bunch of orchids,
Eerie is that I didn't take a step ahead.
In awe that it is again a foul play...

# SWAYAMVAR

A wide hall,
All gazing at a tower tall,
Me felt like for a moment to crawl,
Inside that's me who wants to brawl,
neither because I have lost something,
nor I am about to,
Unquestionably it is a dumb thing…
Wondering what I'm talking about,
Answer to that it is a modern age swayamvar,
An opportunity,
A good chance,
A decent place,
A final destination,
To justify how matches are made in heaven,
And it is not just number seven,
These are the hindu vows,
My education doesn't make me numb for this
Indeed it is a bliss,
It is not a timely indulgence one can enjoy,
It is really not I'm a coy,
Ready to accept the change,
Not ready to surrender my identity,
For the sake of fake creativity,
I want to get adapted with originality,
No matter how long it'll take
My dreams won't be at stake,
Let it be delay,

My mind won't shake,
I'll wait for that diamond,
not for my ring but for my life,
before one morning he'll call ne wife...

# SOLACE

I was with everyone,
Yes, I call these everyone my everyone,
these everyone were the perfect lies,
who happily trusted my smile,
didn't see my cries,
Yes I called these everyone my everyone
startled I were each time they pat me as it just felt on my body,
and didn't reach my soul,
as it wasn't there,
it was out searching for whole…

# THE SWOLLEN PRIDE

Now that the trouble has began,
let it run it's natural course,
your face is red,
the tears you shed,
despairing sobs has made,
your voice hoarse,
yet, never let the dip cross your path,
and sway away the spark,
you still have a beautiful journey to embark…

# SOLDIER AT HOME

The one is that soldier protecting the nation,
the other is inside the porch,
stood strong in every situation,
she hides her tears pain, shortcomings,
in order to run errands successfully,
after seeing us in bliss,
she can sleep peacefully
yet she receives at times the misgivings,
still smiling,
she keeps on admiring,
to the one and all there in the family,
she bears pain beyond her capacity,
a soldier without tag,
the mother,
deserves a salute of gratitude,
right now,
not like that soldier who comes home wrapped in a flag…

# 5 LITTLE THINGS THAT MAKE ME HAPPY

Aren't much,
as such,
it doesn't come after being called a dutchess of a dutch,
it is not holding the grudge,
lifting myself with retouch,
not with make-up but,
a petit trip after a long work,
doing stuff belongs to a jerk,
it's a getaway,
to go faraway,
but to come back in the lap,
oh my mum,
as that trip is a plum,
not available in all seasons,
my mum is above all reasons,
indulgence in a small fist fight,
ya that's true
it is who else,
but him
Whom I call brother,
Rather,
saviour, teacher,
oh la la la
no more appreciation,
it is important for cementation
Ya I found myself as an easy lover,
Yet it is not that I'm a rover,

loved insanely till it is over,
still it is reason of my happiness,
as happiness is a journey,
and no one gets it by signing an attorney,
You, me and us are the foundation,
It is the salvation,
of fears and tears to bound nears and dears.

# "MY SINCEREST APOLOGY"

Apologies are always made
At first for the things done in craze
Now for the words spoken pinched deeper than the blade
In pursuit of life's better plans to be laid
Running faster leaving everything behind in vague
Then again apologies made
For the time lost in theft
None else has done it
Sometimes that is us, only us who is mad in following the parade
Have you ever taken out few moments in jiffs
To thank life to be adorned with ample gifts
Already
For relations you have
Aren't they steady
And ready
To give you hand
And also give you happiness that aren't always planned
So I pondered this time
Took a decision which isn't juvenile
My sincerest apology is
Accepting my life is a bliss
And all those lost hours
I spent in crib and not to devour
The tiny little moments…

www.ingramcontent.com/pod-product-compliance
Lightning Source LLC
Chambersburg PA
CBHW051502140726
47987CB00006B/2844